Spice Mix Recipes

Top 50 Most Delicious Dry Spice Mixes

INTRODUCTION

Spices and herbs, also called seasoning, are an important part of cooking, if not the most important. They can transform an ordinary tasting dish into an incredibly delicious dish. All spices originate from plants. Some are used entirely but some plants have specific parts that are used, like the flowers, roots, barks, leaves, stems and seeds.

Making spice mixes at home is a lot cheaper than buying them in the store, especially when you buy large quantities of them. Just buy a big bag or container of each individual spice and start mixing them at home. Store them in jars and you won't have to buy any spices for years to come. And with the variety of these spice mixes you'll be able to use them for anything and make everything so much more delicious!

Some spices like garlic and cinnamon don't only improve the taste of the dishes but also help in preserving due to their ability to limit bacterial growth. Lots of spices, like turmeric, ginger, garlic, cloves and many more are also very healthy, they contain antioxidants and various other nutrients depending on the spice and herb. They can possess anti-cancer, anti-inflammatory, and immune-boosting properties.

All the recipes in this book are dry spice mixes only and have been categorized according to the region where these spice mixes originated. You'll find spice blends from all over the world, including spice mixes for desserts. So go stock up on some spices and get ready to taste an amazing array of new flavors in your home cooking.

CONTENTS

ITALIAN
SEASONING

PIZZA FLAVOR SPICES AND HERB BLEND

This tasty seasoning can be blended with canned tomato puree to create a pizza sauce or one can simmer this seasoning with tomatoes and with grated cheese can create a marinara sauce.

Yields: Makes five tablespoons seasoning mix

Ingredients

4 tsp of tomato instant bouillon granules
2 1/2 tsp of minced garlic flakes
1 1/2 tsp of dried basil
1 1/2 tsp of minced onion flakes
1 1/2 tsp of dried oregano
1 1/2 tsp of dried rosemary
3/4 tsp of fennel seed
3/4 tsp of dried thyme
1/4 tsp of red pepper flakes
1 tsp of cornstarch
1/2 tsp of ground black pepper
1 tsp of cornstarch (for later use)

Method of Preparation

1. Mix together all the ingredients except the last two in a spice mill or coffee grinder.
2. Process it until the mixture is finely ground.
3. Take the last two ingredients – black pepper and cornstarch and add to the mixture.
4. Seal the container and shake the mixture well.
   Store in a cool and dry place.

ITALIAN SEASONING SALT

This recipe is a wonderful one to create your own salt and use it to flavor so many dishes. The balance of flavors that is found in this salt is worth making and storing for future use.

Yields: 2/3 cup

Ingredients

3 tbsp of garlic powder
3 tbsp of salt
1 tbsp of onion powder
1 tbsp of dried oregano
1 tbsp of dried basil
1 tsp of dried rosemary, crushed
1/2 tsp of black pepper
1/4 tsp of cayenne

Method of Preparation

1. In a jar mix together all the ingredients.
2. Close the lid tightly and shake the jar well for all the ingredients to combine.

ITALIAN STYLE SAUSAGE (GROUND PORK) SEASONING

This mixture is good for two pounds of pork where the casings have been removed and can be stored overnight to blend the flavors well. If you want the mixture to be spicier, add one to two teaspoons of crushed chili flakes.

Yields: Good for two pounds of pork

Ingredients

1 tsp of black pepper
2 tsp of dried parsley
1 1/2 tsp of dried Italian seasoning
1 tsp of garlic powder
1/8 tsp of dried red pepper flakes
3/4 tsp of crushed dried fennel seeds
1/2 tsp of paprika
1 tsp of minced dried onion
2 tsp of salt

Method of Preparation

1. Mix all the ingredients together.
   Store it overnight to let the flavors blend.

ITALIAN SEASONING DRESSING DRY MIX

This all seasoning dry mix is good in pasta salads, spaghetti sauce, or simply sprinkled on fresh, red tomatoes! You can omit salt if you like.

Yields: Makes eight tablespoons

Ingredients

1 1/2 tsp of garlic powder
1 tbsp of onion powder
2 tbsp of oregano leaves
1 tbsp of dried parsley
1 tbsp of granulated sugar
2 tbsp of salt
1 tsp of black pepper
1 tsp of ground basil
1/4 tsp of ground thyme
1/2 tsp of dried celery leaves

Method of Preparation

1. Mix together all the ingredients and store the mixture in an airtight container.

Italian Parmesan Seasoning Mix

This mix can be used in a variety of dishes like pastas, in flour for breading the chicken, in salads, in popcorns and is a delicious mixture to baste hot baked bread with!

Yields: Makes two cups

Ingredients

8 ounce of grated parmesan cheese
3 tbsp of dried Italian seasoning
3 tbsp of dried parsley flakes
1 tbsp of garlic powder
1/2 tsp of ground red pepper

Method of Preparation

1. Mix together all the ingredients and store them in an air tight container or in the refrigerator.

Italian Seasoned Breadcrumbs

This seasoning can be made with day old bread and can be used as stuffing for chicken, peppers, mushrooms, or as a binder for meatballs and meatloaf or can also be used as a coating for shrimp, fish, vegetables and chicken.

Yields: Makes two cups

Ingredients

1 French bread cubed
1/2 tsp of salt
3/4 tsp of parsley flakes
3/4 tsp of oregano
3/4 tsp of dried basil
1/4 tsp of dried rosemary
1/4 tsp of garlic powder
1/4 tsp of onion powder
1/4 tsp of sugar
1/2 cup of parmesan cheese
Optional: 1/4 tsp of crushed red pepper flakes

Method of Preparation

1. Place the bread in a warm oven if the bread is soft so that it dries out or slightly toast the bread.
2. In a food processor, process the bread and add the rest of the ingredients.
3. Store this mixture in ziplock storage bags.

OTHER EUROPEAN SEASONING

HERBES DE PROVENCE

This French Provencal mix is hard to find in stores and most of these mixes have lavender and fennel which haven't been used in this recipe.

Yields: Makes 1/4 cup

Ingredients

1 tsp of dried basil
1 tsp of dried marjoram
1 tsp of dried oregano
1 tbsp of dried rosemary
1 tbsp of dried savory
1 tsp of dried thyme

Method of Preparation

1. Mix together all the ingredients and keep in an airtight container.

FRENCH FOUR SPICE MIX

This mix rarely contains four spices only and can go up to six ingredients. If you want to use this mixture for sweet cooking, then you can go for all spice berries instead of white peppercorns.

Yields: Makes one cup

Ingredients

1 tbsp of white peppercorns
1 small whole nutmeg
10 cloves
1 cinnamon stick
1 tsp of ground ginger

Method of Preparation

1. Mix together all the ingredients in a spice mill and evenly ground them.
    Store the mixture in a dry place.

Sel Fou- French Style Seasoning Salt

This is a seasoning just adds a hint of the flavor of spices sued and does not over power a dish. This seasoning can be used in salads, pastas, soups, pies and hot chips! The corn flour and icing sugar used in this recipe are used as stabilizing agents in this salt.

Yields: Makes a jar

Ingredients

1/3 cup of fine sea salt
1 tbsp of onion salt
1 tbsp of garlic granules
1 tbsp of dried thyme
1 tbsp of dried marjoram
1 tbsp of dried ground horseradish
1/2 tsp of icing sugar
1/2 tsp of corn flour

Method of Preparation

1. Mix together all the ingredients in a large bowl.
    Store the salt in a dry container.

BOUQUET GARNI

This recipe is a perfect gift to give away to your friends and family and the use of tarragon leaves adds flavor to this recipe. This is used for seasoning stews and the bouquet is added in the last 30 minutes of cooking.

Yields: Makes twelve sachets

Ingredients

24 sprigs of fresh parsley
12 bay leaves, divided
1 1/2 tsp of dried whole thyme
1 1/2 tsp of dried tarragon leaves
unbleached muslin cheesecloth
kite string
canning jar

Method of Preparation

1. To make a single bouquet, wrap in a 6 inch square of cheesecloth 2 parsley twigs, 1/8 tsp thyme, 1 bay leaf and 1/8 tsp of tarragon leaves.
2. Using a kite string, tie into a bag.
3. Take a wide mouth jar with a clamped lid and pack the herb bouquets in it.

SPANISH RUB

This lovely spice mix can be used in a number of savory dishes and goes great with chicken and salmon. It can also be a great gift to be given to food enthusiasts.

Yields: Makes about a cup

Ingredients

6 tbsp of smoked paprika
3 tbsp of regular paprika
3 tbsp of dried cilantro
3 tbsp of coarse salt
1 tbsp of ground dried lemon peel
1 1/2 tsp of freshly ground pepper

Method of Preparation

1. Mix together all the ingredients and store it in a jar.

INDIAN SEASONING

TANDOORI SPICE MIX

This mix is a great addition during the barbeque season and this mix can be used in a variety of dishes like chicken, lamb, beef and even shrimp.

Yields: Makes 2/3 cup

Ingredients

3 tbsp of ground ginger
3 tbsp of coriander
1 tbsp of ground cumin
1 tbsp of paprika
1 tbsp of pepper
2 tsp of salt
1 1/2 tsp of turmeric
1 1/2 tsp of ground nutmeg
1 1/2 tsp of ground cloves
1 1/2 tsp of cinnamon

Method of Preparation

1.   Mix together all the ingredients and store it in a container.

GARAM MASALA MIX

The garam masala recipe varies from region to region. This is a basic garam masala recipe that is easy and quick to make.

Yields: Makes three tablespoons

Ingredients

1 tbsp of cardamom seed
1 inch stick of cinnamon bark
1 tsp of whole cumin seed
1 tsp of whole cloves
1 tsp of whole black peppercorn
1/4 tsp of ground nutmeg

Method of Preparation

1.   Place all the ingredients in an electric coffee maker and grind till it turns to powder.

GARAM MASALA KASHMIRI SPICE BLEND

This version of garam masala is slightly longer in its procedure but is a hot and spicy mix which is normally used towards the end of cooking a dish.

Yields: Makes a small jar

Ingredients

30 green cardamom pods, seeds taken from
15 whole cloves
4 cinnamon sticks
5 tbsp of cumin seeds
2 tbsp of coriander seeds
1 tbsp of fennel seed
2 tsp of black peppercorns
1/2 tsp of fenugreek seeds
1/2whole nutmeg, broken into small pieces

Method of Preparation

1. Break the nutmeg into even smaller pieces.
2. Now crush the cardamom seeds using a rolling pin.
3. Take a large frying pan and put all the ingredients in it and stir over low heat.
4. Once the aroma is released, remove the pan from the heat.
5. Take out a small quantity first and blend the mixture in an electric blender.
    Let the mixture cool down and then store it.

PANCH PHORON - THE FIVE SEED SPICE MIXTURE

This is a spice mix from Bengal and roasted meat can be coated with this or it can be used to sprinkle on Indian breads, vegetables especially potatoes, cauliflower and eggplant.

Yields: Makes 3/4 cup

Ingredients

2 tbsp of black mustard seeds
2 tbsp of whole nigella seeds
2 tbsp of cumin seeds
2 tbsp of fenugreek seeds
2 tbsp of fennel seeds

Method of Preparation

1. Mix together all the ingredients and grind them coarsely.

INDIAN RED GUN POWDER

Although the name sounds strange but it is actually called by this name in some parts of India and is a very spicy and hot mixture. It is very tasty and very addictive!

Yields: Makes one serving

Ingredients

1 tsp of vegetable oil
2 tbsp of Bengal gram . Also called channa dal
2 tbsp of white gram beans. Also called urad dal.
15 small dry red chili
1⁄2 tsp of asafetida powder
2 tbsp of sesame seeds
1⁄2 tsp of salt
1 1⁄2 tbsp of brown sugar

Method of Preparation

1. Take a deep skillet and heat oil over medium heat for three minutes.
2. Now add the two dals and chilies.
3. Keep stirring till the dals change their color.
4. Now stir in the sesame seeds and asafetida.
5. Continue to fry the mixture till a lovely roasted aroma comes out.
6. Now let the mixture cool in a plate.
7. Add salt and sugar to the mixture.
8. Take a coffee grinder and grind the mixture to powder. The powder should have a grainy texture.

SAMBAR PODI

Podi means powder in English and this is a spice from Southern India. This later evolved into British style curry powder

Yields: Makes 2/3 cup

Ingredients

3 tbsp of ground coriander
3 tbsp of chickpea
1 tbsp of ground cumin
1 1/2 tsp of fresh coarse ground black pepper
1 tsp of salt
1 tsp of ground fenugreek
1 tsp of amchur powder
1 tsp of dry mustard
1 tsp of hot red chili powder
1/2 tsp of ground cinnamon
1/2 tsp of turmeric
8 crumbled dried curry leaves
1/4 tsp of asafetida powder

Method of Preparation

1. Mix together all the ingredients and grind them in a coffee grinder. Store in a cool and dry place.

CHAAT MASALA

This is an absolute favorite in all Indian homes and can be used as a seasoning in a fruit salad or for any other dish as a garnish. It peps up the flavor!

Yields: Makes 1/4 small jar

Ingredients

6 tsp of cumin seeds, lightly roasted for a minute and then ground
3 tsp of amchur powder (dried raw mango powder)
2 tsp of black salt
1/2 tsp of white salt
1 tsp of paprika

Method of Preparation

1. Mix all the ingredients and store it in a jar for future use.

BIRYANI SPICES MIX

The spice mix is used in traditional rice and meat dish and is goes well with the non-vegetarian curries. It is medium hot in flavor and adds taste to the curries.

Yields: Makes 2 1/2 cups

Ingredients

1/4 cup of ground red chili powder
1/4 cup of ground paprika
1 tbsp of turmeric
1/4 cup of salt
1 tbsp of garlic powder
1 tbsp of ginger powder
2 tbsp of roasted ground cumin
1 tbsp of ground aniseed
1 tbsp of pepper
1 tbsp of star ground aniseed
1 tsp of ground cinnamon
1 tbsp of ground black cardamom pod
1 tsp of ground black cumin seeds
1 tsp of ground cloves
1 tbsp of ground green cardamoms
1/2 tbsp of ground mace
1/2 tbsp of ground nutmeg
3 bay leaves, torn
1 cup of dried apricot
1/2 cup of roasted coriander seed, ground

Method of Preparation

1. Mix together all the ingredients and store it in a cool and dry place.

INDIAN SPICE MIX

This spice mix goes well as a dressing for various dishes. It has a nice spicy and sweet flavor to it and the combination of different spices makes it a well-balanced spice mix.

Yields: Makes seven tablespoons

Ingredients

2 tbsp of curry
2 tbsp of cumin
2 tsp of turmeric
2 tsp of ground coriander
1 tsp of ground ginger
1/2 tsp of ground cardamom
1/2 tsp of ground cinnamon

Method of Preparation

1. Mix together all the ingredients and store it in a jar for future use.

ASIAN SEASONINGS

GOMASHI (TOASTED SESAME SALT)

This is a macrobiotic seasoning and is said to reduce acidity in the blood. It improves indigestion and is believed to heal all blood related diseases.

Yields: Makes two cups

Ingredients

2 cups of unhulled brown sesame seeds
3 tbsp of sea salt

Method of Preparation

1. Take a heavy skillet and toast the sea salt until it turns grey. Remove it from the skillet and keep it aside.
2. Now toast the sesame seeds till they turn brown and start popping.
3. Now put the salt and the seeds in a blender and they should only be 95% crushed.
Do not refrigerate but keep it in a jar in a cool and dry place.

Xinjiang Spice Mix

This spice mix can be used in sautés, barbecues, roasts or whatever you feel like adding it to. Since it's a very fragrant mixture it will is a delight to one's senses.

Yields: Makes six to ten servings

Ingredients

1/4 cup of cumin seeds
2 tbsp of dried szechuan chile flakes
2 tbsp of black pepper
1 tbsp of szechuan peppercorns
1 tbsp of ground ginger powder
1 tbsp of garlic powder
1 1/2 tsp of chili powder
1 1/2 tsp of sea salt

Method of Preparation

1. Toast cumin seeds and Sichuan peppercorns for some time.
2. Grind the cumin seeds, black pepper, chili flakes and the peppercorns in a spice grinder.
    Add the remaining ingredients to the mixture and store it.

CHINESE FIVE- SPICE POWDER

Although this mixture is available in the markets, making it at home adds more flavor and fragrance to this lovely spice mixture. It adds a touch of home to your dish.

Yields: Makes two tablespoons

Ingredients

1 tsp of ground cinnamon
1 tsp of ground cloves
1 tsp of fennel seed, toasted and ground
1 tsp of ground star anise
1 tsp of szechuan peppercorns, toasted and ground

Method of Preparation

1. Mix together all the spices and store them in a jar.

SPICED PANKO BREAD CRUMBS

This exciting recipe uses basil, thyme, chili and ginger to flavor these bread crumbs. You can even add cayenne powder and make it spicier.

Yields: Makes four cups

Ingredients

4 cups panko breadcrumbs
2 tbsp of dried thyme
2 tbsp of dried basil
1 tbsp of powdered ginger
1 tbsp of fresh coarse ground black pepper
1 tbsp of chili powder

Method of Preparation

1. Mix together all the ingredients and store them in a dry place.

Shichimi Togarashi (Japanese Seven Spice)

This spicy-savory blend enhances the flavor of noodles and grilled meats. It can even be used to sprinkle over avocado and popcorn!

Yields: Makes a jar

Ingredients

1 tbsp of black peppercorns
1 tbsp of dried tangerine peel
2tsp of flaked nori
1 tbsp of ground red chilli pepper
2tsp of white poppy seeds
2 tsp of black sesame seeds
2 tsp of minced garlic

Method of Preparation

1. Mix together all the ingredients and store in an airtight container.

AFRICAN SEASONING

NORTH AFRICAN RAS EL HANOUT SPICE MIX

The original recipe uses around 50 spices but in this recipe we have incorporated the main traditional spices which are easily and readily available.

Yields: Makes one jar

Ingredients

3 tsp of ground cinnamon
3 tsp of ground cumin
3 tsp of ground turmeric
2 tsp of ground coriander
2 tsp of ground ginger
2 tsp of ground cardamom
1 tsp of ground nutmeg
1 tsp of ground cloves
1 tsp of mace
1 tsp of cayenne pepper
1 tsp of garlic powder
1 tsp of ground celery seed
1 tsp of ground black pepper
2 tsp of corn flour

Method of Preparation

1. Mix all the spices together and store them in a container.

SOUTH AFRICAN SPICE MIXTURE

This spice mix is a mixture of sweet and pungent spices but creates a wonderful mixture. It is mildly hot and can be used in all types of curries.

Yields: Makes one large jar

Ingredients

1 tbsp of clove
1/2 cup of coriander seed
1 tbsp of fennel seed
1 tbsp of black mustard seeds
3 tbsp of fenugreek seeds
2 tbsp of black peppercorns
3 small dried hot red chilies
3 tbsp of cumin seeds
1/4 cup of ground cardamom
1/4 cup of ground turmeric
1 tbsp of ground ginger
2 curry leaves, chopped into small pieces

Method of Preparation

1. In a frying pan roast all the seeds for a minute or two.
2. Take a food processor and finely ground the mixture.
3. Now add the remaining spices and mix well.
   Store in an airtight container.

DUKKA- EGYPTIAN MIX

This mixture of spices and nuts can be taken as a snack or an appetizer and you can drizzle olive oil over the mixture and have it.

Yields: Makes one cup

Ingredients

1 cup of almonds or hazelnuts
1/3 cup of whole coriander seed
3 tbsp of cumin seeds
1 tsp of kosher salt or sea salt
2 tbsp of sumac
1/4 cup of toasted sesame seeds

Method of Preparation

1. Preheat oven to 350 degrees and toast the almonds on a baking sheet for five to seven minutes.
2. Take a large skillet and toast coriander, salt and cumin for three minutes over low heat.
3. Mix together all the ingredients except the sesame seeds and process them in a food processor.
   Once the mixture in done, ass the sesame seeds and store in an airtight container.

AFRICAN CURRY POWDER

This mixture can be used in chicken or beef. This homemade spice mix taste much better than the store brought mixes.

Yields: Makes one cup

Ingredients

6 tsp of ground ginger
6 tsp of dried garlic
4 tbsp of ground coriander
4 tbsp of ground cumin
4 tbsp of ground turmeric
2 tsp of cayenne
2 tsp of hot chili powder

Method of Preparation

1. Mix together all the spices and store it in a cool and dry place.

BERBERE SPICE MIX

This Ethiopian spice mix can be used to season chicken, grilled fish or meat while cooking and can be used to sprinkle over vegetables and meat.

Yields: Makes 1/3 cup

Ingredients

8 tsp of chile powder or 2 tbsp of cayenne pepper
5 tsp of sweet paprika
1 tbsp of salt
1 tsp of ground coriander
1/2 tsp of ground ginger
3/8 tsp of ground cardamom
3/8 tsp of ground fenugreek
1/4 tsp of ground nutmeg
1/4 tsp of ground allspice
1/8 tsp of ground cloves

Method of Preparation

1. Mix together all the ingredients and store them in a dry and cool place.

MIDDLE EASTERN SEASONING

ARABIC SEVEN SPICE

A very easy to make recipe, this adds flavor to your food and can be bought at stores but to make it from the scratch adds a distinctive flavor which you will not find in readymade grocery options.

Yields: Makes 1/2 cup

Ingredients

2 tbsp of ground black pepper
2 tbsp of paprika
2 tbsp of ground cumin
1 tbsp of ground coriander
1 tbsp of ground cloves
1 tsp of ground nutmeg
1 tsp of ground cinnamon
1/2 tsp of ground cardamom

Method of Preparation

1. Mix all the ingredients and store them in an air tight container.

SAUDI KASBA SPICE MIX

A lovely combination of spices, it is easy to make and packed with flavors. The whole spices make it flavorful and aromatic and can be used in any dish.

Yields: Makes six tablespoons

Ingredients

1 tsp of turmeric
1 tsp of coriander seed
1 tsp of black peppercorns
1 tsp of black cardamom pod
1 tsp of ginger
1 tsp of fennel seed

Method of Preparation

1. Blend the mixture until crushed.

MIXED SPICES MIX- BAHARAT

A lovely blend of mixed spices, this recipe is suited for those who would love to get a authentic taste of the mid-eastern.

Yields: Makes two cups

Ingredients

1/2 cup of whole black peppercorn
1/4 cup of whole coriander seed
1/4 cup of cinnamon bark
1/4 cup of whole cloves
1/3 cup of cumin seed
2 tsp of whole cardamom seeds
4 whole nutmegs
1/2 cup of ground paprika

Method of Preparation

1. Except for nutmeg and paprika, put all the remaining ingredients in a blender and process it till it turn to powder.
2. Add paprika and grated nutmeg into the spices. Since nutmeg is toxic in large doses, be careful of how much you use.

MOROCCAN SPICE RUB

This spice is well suited for all kinds of meat and can be added to the lamb or leg of a lamb for an extra flavor. You can even sprinkle this mix on potatoes.

Yields: Makes five tablespoons

Ingredients

2 tbsp of ground cumin
1 tbsp of paprika
1 tbsp of ground coriander
1 tsp of salt
1 tsp of fresh ground black pepper
1 tsp of cinnamon
1 tsp of allspice
1/4 tsp of clove
1/8 tsp of cayenne, to taste

Method of Preparation

1. Mix together all the ingredients and store in a dry and cool place.

SHOARMA SPICE MIX

This spice mix when made at home adds a unique flavor to your chicken and meats. It tastes delicious unlike the readymade ones you will get at the stores. This mix does not include salt so add that when use this spice mix for cooking.

Yields: Makes one small jar

Ingredients

1 tbsp of ground cumin
1 tbsp of ground coriander
1 tbsp of garlic powder
1/2 tbsp of paprika
1 tsp of turmeric powder
1/2 tsp of ground cloves
1/2 tsp of ground cayenne pepper
1 tsp of ground ginger
1 tsp of ground black pepper
1/2 tsp of ground cinnamon

Method of Preparation

1. Mix together all the ingredients and store them in a container.

MEXICAN SEASONING

DRY ENCHILADA SAUCE MIX

This is a great mix of spices and is a unique way of storing the mix without having to worry about its shelf life.

Yields: Makes 1 1/2 ounces

Ingredients

2 tsp of mild chili powder
2 tsp of paprika
2 tsp of cornstarch
1 1/2 tsp of salt
1 1/2 tsp of dried onion flakes
1 tsp of sugar
1 tsp of ground cumin
1 tsp of garlic powder
1/2 tsp of oregano
1/2 tsp of ground coriander
1/4 tsp of cayenne

Method of Preparation

1. Mix together all the ingredients and store them in a dry place.

TACO SEASONING MIX

A delightful seasoning and contains no sugar in it. This recipe is an all-time favorite and can be sued whenever you make those tacos.

Yields: Makes one package

Ingredients

2 tsp of instant onion, minced
1 tsp of chili powder
1/2 tsp of crushed dried red pepper
1/4 tsp of dried oregano
1 tsp of salt
1/2 tsp of cornstarch
1/2 tsp of instant garlic, minced
1/2 tsp of ground cumin

Method of Preparation

1. Mix together all the ingredients and store them in cool and dry place.

Fajita Seasoning Mix

Here is another mix that is bound to make you its loyal follower. This mix uses all the healthy ingredients and is much better than the readymade seasoning mix that you will find in your grocery stores.

Yields: Makes ten teaspoons

Ingredients

1 tbsp of cornstarch
2 tsp of chili powder
1 tsp of salt
1 tsp of paprika
1 tsp of sugar
3⁄4 tsp of crushed chicken bouillon cube
1⁄2 tsp of onion powder
1⁄4 tsp of garlic powder
1⁄4 tsp of cayenne pepper
1⁄4 tsp of cumin

Method of Preparation

1. Mix all the ingredients and store them in a cool and dry place.

CHILI SEASONING MIX

Most of the times when are cooking something that requires chili, we run out of our seasoning packets. This recipe is easy and quick to make and adds a great flavor to your dish.

Yields: Makes 1/4 cup

Ingredients

1 tbsp of white flour, unbleached
1 1/2 tsp of chili powder
1/2 tsp of red pepper flakes, crushed
1/2 tsp of sugar
2 tbsp of dried onion
1 tsp of seasoning salt
1/2 tsp of dried garlic
1/2 tsp of ground cumin

Method of Preparation

1. Mix together all the ingredients and store them in a dry place.

ADOBO SEASONING

This is a great recipe to make and one can store it and use it as and when required. You can simply sprinkle this seasoning on chicken, cottage cheese, and fish. Enjoy!

Yields: Makes seven tablespoons

Ingredients

2 tbsp of salt
1 tbsp of paprika
2 tsp of ground black pepper
1 1/2 tsp of onion powder
1 1/2 tsp of dried oregano
1 1/2 tsp of ground cumin
1 tsp of garlic powder
1 tsp of chili powder

Method of Preparation

1. Mix together all the ingredients and store them for future use.

NORTH AMERICAN SEASONING

Cajun Seasoning Mix

Once you make this mix at home you will never go and buy the mix from stores. This mix is delicious and is not at all salty or uses any unnecessary ingredients.

Yields: Makes four tablespoons

Ingredients

2 tsp of white pepper
2 tsp of garlic powder
2 tsp of onion powder
2 tsp of cayenne pepper
2 tsp of paprika
2 tsp of ground black pepper

Method of Preparation

1. Process all the ingredients in a food processor and store in an air tight container.

BBQ SPICE RUB

This is a very simple and easy spice to make. It can be used in nearly everything – be it chicken, pork, steak or even burgers. It can be stored and used for months.

Yields: Makes 1 1/4 cup

Ingredients

1/2 cup of brown sugar
1/2 cup of paprika
1 tbsp of ground black pepper
1 tbsp of chili powder
1 tbsp of garlic powder
1 tbsp of onion powder
1 tbsp of salt
Optional: 1 tsp of cayenne pepper

Method of Preparation

1. Mix all the ingredients together and store them in an air tight container.

OLD BAY SEASONING

This recipe is traditionally used for seasoning steamed crabs but this recipe has been modified to be used on potato salads, other vegetables as well as fish.

Yields: Makes half a cup

Ingredients

2 tbsp of bay leaf powder
2 tbsp of celery salt
1 tbsp of dry mustard
2 tsp of ground black pepper
2 tsp of ground ginger
2 tsp of sweet paprika
1 tsp of white pepper
1 tsp of ground nutmeg
1 tsp of ground cloves
1 tsp of ground allspice
1/2 tsp of crushed red pepper flakes
1/2 tsp of ground mace
1/2 tsp of ground cardamom
1/4 tsp of ground cinnamon

Method of Preparation

1. Mix together all the ingredients and store them in an air tight container.

POULTRY SEASONING

This poultry seasoning uses all the ingredients that are cheap and easy to make. It is an all-time favorite when it comes to using it for all the poultry dishes.

Yields: Makes an ounce

Ingredients

2 tsp of ground sage
1 1/2 tsp of ground thyme
1 tsp of ground marjoram
3/4 tsp of ground rosemary
1/2 tsp of nutmeg
1/2 tsp of finely ground black pepper

Method of Preparation

1.   Mix together all the ingredients and store it in a cool and dry place.

DESSERT SPICE MIXES

Dutch Speculaas Spice Mix

A lot of sweet Dutch recipes require this warm spice mix called 'speculaaskruiden' and it consists of a harmony of beautifully smelling spices that add a delicious flavor to desserts, cookies, bread, cake, pie crust and whatever you can think of. Add a little Dutch to your goodies and experiment. The optional ingredients are flavors that you can add on top of that, they are known to blend well with the original recipe and create new unique flavors. You can play around with the quantities.

Yields: Makes one jar

Ingredients

Original recipe:
2 tbsp of ground cinnamon
1/2 tsp of nutmeg
1/2 tsp of ground ginger
1/2 tsp of ground cloves
1/2 teaspoon of ground anise
1/4 tsp of cardamom
1/4 tsp of mace
1/4 tsp of white ground pepper

Extra additions:
1/4 teaspoon of orange zest (optional)
1/4 teaspoon of ground coriander seed (optional)
1/4 teaspoon of allspice (optional)

Method of Preparation

1. Mix together all the ingredients and store in an airtight jar.

PUMPKIN PIE SPICE

This is such a lovely addition to Pumpkin Pie that it makes it more delicious. It is difficult to find this spice preparation in the stores and best made at home. It can be used when making cookies.

Yields: Makes 5oz

Ingredients

1/4 cup of ground cinnamon
1/8 cup of ground ginger
1 tbsp of nutmeg
1 tbsp of ground cloves

Method of Preparation

1. Mix together all the ingredients and shake well before use.

FIVE SPICE SUGAR

This lovely concoction can be used on almost anything. It is a good substitute for Splenda. This is a versatile addition for anything!

Yields: Makes five to six tablespoons

Ingredients

5 tbsp of sugar
1/2-1 tsp of ground cinnamon
1/2 tsp of ground nutmeg
1/2 tsp of ground ginger
1/2 tsp of ground cardamom
1/2 tsp of ground coriander

Method of Preparation

1. Stir all these spices together and store.

ORANGE SPICE BLEND

You can use this preparation in cake batter, whipped cream etc. Instead of orange rind you can use lemon peel if you like.

Yields: Makes six tablespoons

Ingredients

2 tbsp of ground cinnamon
1 tbsp of ground nutmeg
1 1/2 tsp of ground cloves
1 1/2 tsp of ground allspice
1 tbsp of ground ginger
1 tbsp of orange zest

Method of Preparation

1. Mix together all the ingredients and store in a cool and dry place.

APPLE PIE SPICE

This simple recipe can be mixed with breadcrumbs when making breaded pork chops or simply sprinkled on a buttered toast!

Yields: Makes 1/4 cup

Ingredients

1/4 cup of cinnamon
2 tsp of nutmeg
1 tsp of allspice
1 tsp of ground ginger

Method of Preparation

1. Mix together all the ingredients and store them in a cool place.

GINGERBREAD SPICE MIXTURE

This mixture is versatile enough to be used in cakes, cookies, pancake or waffle batter, muffins, in ground coffee before brewing and you can even season custards with this!

Yields: Makes one 3/4 cup

Ingredients

1/2 cup of cinnamon
1/2 cup of ground ginger
1/4 cup of allspice
1/4 cup of nutmeg
1/4 cup of ground cloves

Method of Preparation

1. Mix together all the ingredients and store it in a cool and dry place.

Printed in Great Britain
by Amazon

42807810R00040